THE SOU⌐
W

The Long Man of Wilmington – at 235ft the largest chalk figure in England.

David Harrison

S.B. Publications

By the same author
Exploring Eastbourne and the South Downs
Exploring Brighton and the South Downs
Exploring Ashdown Forest

To Tony Freeman, who also loves the South Downs

First published in 2002 by S. B. Publications,
19 Grove Road, Seaford, East Sussex BN25 1TP

ISBN 1 85770 161 5

Maps by Map Creation, Woodlands Park Avenue, Woodlands Park,
Maidenhead. SL6 3LT.

Designed and typeset by CGB, Lewes. Tel: 01273 476622
Printed by Page Turn Ltd. Units 2 & 3 Sussex Industrial Estate,
Old Shoreham Road, Hove BN3 7EG. Tel 01273-821500

CONTENTS

Front cover: The South Downs Way at Ditchling Beacon. Photo: Graham Thorton, Crawley.

ABOUT THE AUTHOR

David Harrison was born in Doncaster, Yorkshire in May 1943, son of a railwayman. A move to Kent in 1970 started his interest in rambling, with the North Downs Way and the Pilgrims' Way offering an ideal opportunity to explore the northern parts of that county. Business commitments in Cambridgeshire gave him the chance to walk much of East Anglia before making his home in Sussex in 1987. There his successful newsagent's business brought him into constant touch with visitors seeking advice on places of interest and walks in the area and, since his first book *Exploring Eastbourne and the South Downs* was published in 1995, subsequent projects have had him  walking the South Downs on a regular basis. He is now retired – and still walking.

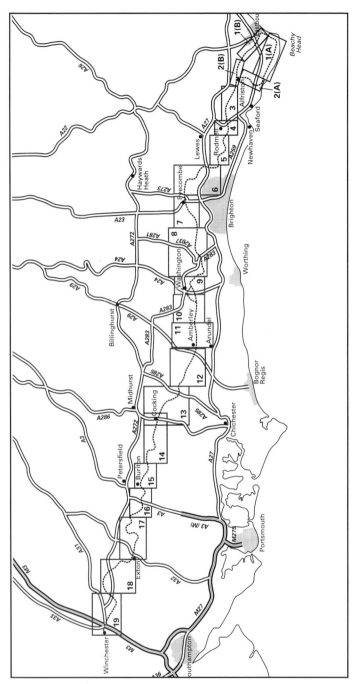

The South Downs Way, showing the map sections between Eastbourne and Winchester.

How to use this Guide

Identify the route you intend to take and find the starting point on the sketch map (not to scale) on the page facing the start of the appropriate section.

Directions are given as simply and as straightforwardly as possible and it should be easy to follow the route as each successive mile is indicated on the sketch maps to help you determine exactly where you are. A Landranger Ordnance Survey map would also help in this respect, but is not essential.

Parking areas **P,** and places where refreshments and toilets are available **PH,** are indicated on each sketch map, as are the names of the landmarks referred to in the text.

Places of interest in the vicinity of the Way are indicated by letters of the alphabet on the maps and a description of them given at the end of each section of the route, together with the addresses and telephone numbers of B&B accommodation and camping, stabling and grazing facilities available at the time of going to press.

All this information was correct at the time of publication but it is advisable to telephone ahead to check availability and opening times before venturing any distance from the route.

The cliffs of the Seven Sisters showing the great depth of the chalk deposits.

The South Downs

The creation of the Downs began many millions of years ago with volcanoes and earth movements forming a platform of Palaeozoic rocks. Through time this platform acted as the foundation for a series of sedimentary deposits from the waters of a great freshwater lake which, through pressure, were consolidated into rock strata. Then the land slowly sank allowing the sea to flood the area and a chalky sediment appeared, much of it from the shells of minute sea creatures called *Foraminifera* which sank to the bottom as they ended their short lives, their soft bodies dissolving and leaving the detritus of their shells to add to the build up of chalk. This was known as the Cretaceous period which lasted a long time for the beds of chalk it created were hundreds of metres thick.

The Eocene period followed, when deposits of sand and clay covered the chalk also to a considerable depth. Vast earth movements brought this peaceful deposition period to an abrupt end, resulting in the Alps in central Europe and creating a huge dome stretching from France to Hampshire and back as far as the North Downs in Kent. With the sedimentary strata now exposed to erosion from the wind and rain our present Downs landscape developed. The incursion of the sea which formed the English Channel breached the chalk hills exposing sheer cliffs where the thickness of the chalk deposits are well demonstrated. Perfect examples of this can be seen at Beachy Head and all along the Seven Sisters.

The South Downs Way was one of six long-distance footpaths initiated in 1947 by a special committee on Footpaths and Access to the Countryside. It was originally intended that the route should stretch from Eastbourne, where the South Downs start, to Winchester, where it would join the Pilgrims Way and continue to a point west of Salisbury.

Fifteen years later the National Parks Commission, predecessor to the Countryside Commission, submitted a proposal to the Minister of Housing and Local Government for the route to stretch from Eastbourne to the West Sussex county boundary near Buriton, and this was approved the following year.

On 15 July 1972 the South Downs Way was officially opened by Lord Shawcross, albeit with an alternative route, the footpath following the cliffs over Beachy Head and the Seven Sisters to Cuckmere Haven and from there over the hills to join the original route near Alfriston.

The Way is by no means a new route. The greater part of it was already in existence when the special committee was deliberating long-distance footpaths back in 1947. Much of it is ancient trackway, now accessible to man and horse along its entirety. Waymarkers of various kinds direct the user. In a number of instances these bear the acorn sign – the Commission's long distance route symbol.

Be prepared to experience a variety of extraordinary sensations along the South Downs Way. The views from some of the ridges almost give one the sensation of flying yet the approaches to them are often simple and gentle ascents. There is an incredible feeling of space, of silence and of solitude – yet the bustle of civilisation is but a few miles away at most. Because of the underlying chalk bed the route is seldom affected by the wettest of

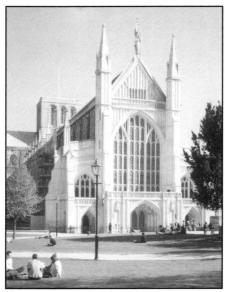

Winchester Cathedral

weather and, as the Way is maintained so well, the paths are not impassable at any season of the year.

It is best to travel the route from east to west for two reasons. Winchester makes a wonderful finish – the feeling of fulfilment endorsed by the majesty of the ancient Saxon capital of England – and it can be done in this direction in daylight hours without having to face the full glare of the sun.

The Way is 105 miles (170km) long. It needs at least five days to cover the entire length but it would be better to allow seven or even eight days in order to digest all the interesting features it has to offer.

Walking the Way is like passing through history. Many features of the landscape, for example Combe Hill above Jevington and Barkhale on Bignor Hill, date from the Neolithic period, *c*3000BC. Around 2500BC burial chambers in the form of round barrows appeared on the Downs and a thousand years later came the Bronze Age settlements and the formation of the trackways which were the trade routes between them. With the Iron Age more elaborate hill forts were built and evidence of them is still to be seen at Devil's Dyke, on Cissbury Ring and Old Winchester Hill.

The Romans saw the Downs as a strategic bridgehead for the conquest of Britain and the remains of Stane Street – their main route from Chichester to London – are on Bignor Hill.

Looking across the meanders of the Cuckmere to the site of the lost village of Exceat.

The Anglo-Saxons were responsible for a number of simple churches built of local materials, such as the round-towered one at Southease. The Normans, who followed them, built more imposing edifices for an expanding population and there are many examples of their work in villages along the Way. However, the Black Death of 1348-49 halved the country's population of four million and many of the new churches, their congregations desperately depleted, became derelict and villages such as Exceat in the Cuckmere Valley and Lomer on Preshaw Down, were deserted altogether.

The survivors continued to cultivate their crops in small fields and the flocks of sheep that were to make the Southdown breed famous for delicious lamb and mutton grazed freely on the springy green turf. Two world wars did much to alter the appearance of the Downs. The turf on which sheep grazed was ploughed up to grow food crops in large fenced fields and in the inter-war years there was an increasing amount of housing development. It was the Town and Country Planning Act of 1947 that brought speculative building under control and preserved for posterity much of the natural beauty of the Downs.

Preparing to walk the Way

Depending on the time of year, dress accordingly. In winter the winds can be bitingly cold so a warm, waterproof hat or hood is essential along with a lightweight, windproof and watertight jacket. Waterproof trousers or leggings are essential but jeans and clothes of a similar material are not a good idea, they become very heavy and cumbersome when wet and can hinder progress and cause reduced body temperature very quickly. In summer be sure to wear a long sleeved shirt to protect the arms from sunburn; there is little protection along certain stretches of the Way even from the sun.

Plan each day's route beforehand, especially if you intend travelling for several days at a time. Each of the sections of this guide provide for a good day's walking, bearing in mind it will not all be on a level surface and taking into consideration places of interest you may wish to visit along the route. Riders of horses or bicycles will obviously be able to cover greater daily distances and this should be taken into consideration when arranging accommodation.

Remember that several thousand people use the South Downs Way every week so the need to book accommodation in advance is essential. Youth hostels, in particular, get full very quickly so early booking is advisable. With such a vast number of visitors each year it is surprising how the Way avoids congestion. The more popular areas can be busy in summer, however, especially the Seven Sisters, Alfriston, Devil's Dyke, Queen Elizabeth Country Park and Old Winchester Hill, so be prepared for the occasional crush.

Camping along the Way is not permitted but there are several camp sites off the route and most farmers, if approached, are likely to give permission to camp on their land.

Always carry a drink – water in summer and a hot drink in winter. There are water points along the route but dehydration can occur quickly and should be dealt with immediately. A simple first aid kit is essential – plasters for blisters, crepe bandage for sprains and so on.

A mobile phone is the hi-tech equivalent of the walkers' traditional help-summoning device – the whistle. Take them both and if the mobile 'phone is damaged or has a flat battery the recognised distress signal is six sharp blasts of the whistle and three in reply. Sound carries far on the Downs and help in an emergency summoned in this way should arrive reasonably quickly.

A torch is handy if making use of overnight accommodation and a lightweight haversack should be sufficient to carry all this equipment without incommoding the walker.

Do please observe the Country Code:

- Guard against risk of fire
- Fasten all gates
- Keep dogs under proper control
- Keep to the paths across farmland
- Avoid damaging fences, hedges and walls
- Do not leave any litter. Take it home
- Do not pollute any water supplies such as dewponds and cattle troughs
- Do nothing that will harm the wildlife, or damage plants and trees
- Take particular care on country roads

The Way can be hard going in places especially when the path is pitted with flints. A good strong pair of walking boots will make the going a lot easier but be sure to wear them in beforehand otherwise blisters can be guaranteed.

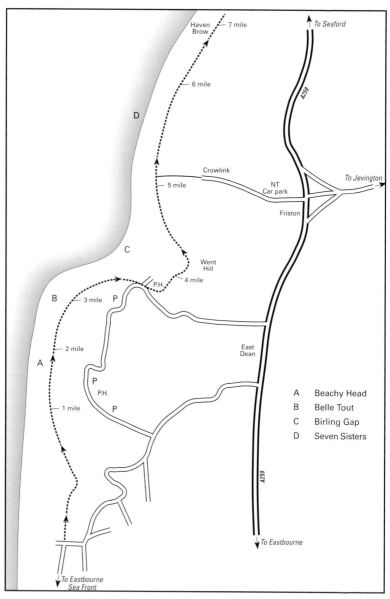

Haven Brow — 7 mile

To Seaford

6 mile

D

A259

Crowlink

5 mile

NT Car park

To Jevington

Friston

C

Went Hill

P.H. — 4 mile

B — 3 mile   P

East Dean

2 mile

A

P

P.H.

A   Beachy Head
B   Belle Tout
C   Birling Gap
D   Seven Sisters

1 mile   P

A259

To Eastbourne

To Eastbourne Sea Front

EASTBOURNE to HAVEN BROW – 7 miles.

Section 1

EASTBOURNE to ALFRISTON
Footpath section – 11 miles (17.2km)

At the western end of the promenade by Holywell Retreat begin with a steep climb, up some steps and then on to the acorn marker post where fork right, then left at the second post. Follow the waymarkers along a track as far as an open clearing where keep left at the concrete footpath sign then continue along a narrow path to Beachy Head (**A**). Seaward is Whitbread Hole with its playing field in the dip.

Pass the small octagonal brick enclosure, which is all that remains of a Lloyds signal station, and the public house and restaurant with its small museum, before continuing along the undulating cliff top as far as Belle Tout (**B**).

The Way passes along the inland wall enclosure, descending towards the old coastguard look-out station before dropping down into Birling Gap (**C**) with its hotel and relevant amenities.

From Birling Gap set off up the hill along a gravel track with a South Downs Way sign showing the route behind the hotel. Turn right along a path before turning left along the line of the open cliffs at Went Hill and the start of the Seven Sisters (**D**), passing the sarsen stone commemorating the purchase by public subscription of Crowlink valley in 1926.

> The well-defined path leading off right at Gap Bottom in the next dip leads to the hamlet of Crowlink, the one-time home of E. Nesbit who wrote *The Railway Children*. This was once a busy working estate but the buildings that nestle snugly in the valley are now mostly private dwellings or holiday homes.
>
> There is access to A259 at Friston church and buses to Eastbourne and Brighton.

From the top of Haven Brow, the last of the Seven Sisters, there are splendid views across the Cuckmere Valley, the only natural and unspoilt river estuary in the south east, with the River Cuckmere weaving its way up the valley to Exceat Bridge and the straight channel that was cut in 1846 to bypass the meanders to prevent flooding.

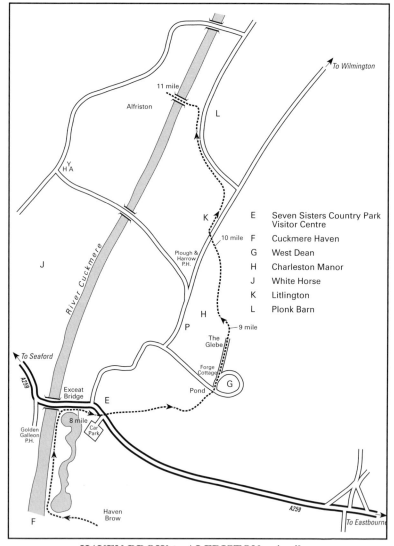

HAVEN BROW to ALFRISTON – 4 miles.

Follow a wire fence on the right to a stile halfway down the hill, keeping to a steep chalk path to where a South Downs Way plinth directs the route across the shingle beach before following the straight river along its east bank to Exceat Bridge.

The Golden Galleon over the bridge has refreshments.

The main route turns right along the footpath alongside the A259 as far as the Seven Sisters Country Park Visitor Centre (**E**) where there are bus stops for Eastbourne, Seaford and Brighton. Cross the road by the car park, continuing past one of the centre's buildings where bicycles are available for hire and where an acorn sign confirms the route.

Over the stile and straight up the field ahead, crossing the stile in the wall from where there are magnificent views back across Cuckmere Haven (**F**). Turn right over the wall, then left at the acorn marker post, descending the long staircase to West Dean (**G**). Pass the pond on the left, continuing ahead past Forge Cottage.

To take the short detour round the village, turn right at the road, rejoining the main route back at Forge Cottage.

Keep right at the Glebe, climb over the stile and turn left at the yellow waymarker signposted Litlington. Cross a stile to descend rough steps to the rear of Charleston Manor (**H**) of which only a glimpse is possible.

Pass over the drive and along a narrow path before turning sharp right over a stile. Follow a rising path along the borders of three fields before crossing two more stiles from where there is an uninterrupted view of the White Horse (**J**) cut into the side of High and Over.

Keep beside the right edge of the next field then down an obvious path to a kissing gate through which turn left at the metalled road then right into Litlington (K).

Follow the road through the village to the church where a path suddenly appears taking the route past three houses called Ham before entering a field over a stile. The route is obvious from here as far as Plonk Barn (**L**), where turn left over the bridge into Alfriston.

POINTS OF INTEREST

(A) Beachy Head

The 575 feet (175m) sea cliff might not be the highest in Britain but it is certainly the best known and most visited. The name Beachy is derived from the French *beau chef* meaning 'noble headland'. The Head, along with the clifftop of the Seven Sisters, is under the protection of the National Trust and the Forestry Commission.

In 1924 Eastbourne Borough Council bought 1,600 hectares and in 1957 acquired a further 40 hectares. The council was given Whitbread Hollow in 1920. Mesolithic and Neolithic remains have been found in the area, confirming that man has inhabited the Downs since about 12000BC.

Refreshments and toilet facilities are available here.

(B) Belle Tout

This lighthouse was built in 1831 by 'Mad Jack' Fuller, an eccentric Sussex ironmaster with a fondness for building follies.

It was frequently fog-bound, perched as it was high on the cliffs, and it was replaced in 1902 by Trinity House with the red-banded lighthouse at the foot of Beachy Head. Belle Tout was advertised for sale as 'a substantial three-storey building' and has, since the Second World War, had a variety of owners and been the location for several films. Its most recent television appearance was when it was lifted and moved back from the crumbling edge of the cliff.

Belle Tout lighthouse.

The Seven Sisters, ending with Haven Brow at the Cuckmere estuary.

(C) Birling Gap

There is a car park here, a few cottages huddled on the hillside, an hotel and a row of coastguard cottages which have survived from the nineteenth century. There is little else save for a beach and access to some of the finest sea cliffs in Britain.

> Birling Gap Hotel, built in 1887, offers B&B with en suite facilities, a carvery, pub food and Sussex cream teas. Tel: 01323-423197

(D) Seven Sisters

This famous stretch of sea cliffs, 2.75 miles (4.5km) long, offers some of the most magnificent coastal scenery in Britain. There are, in fact, eight crests, but they are always known by their familiar alliterative name.

The first is Went Hill which drops down into Michel Dean, then up to Baileys Hill where there is an obelisk marking the gift of land by W A Robertson to the National Trust. Next comes Flat Hill – the 'sister' usually excluded to make the famous seven – dropping down into Flagstaff Bottom, then up to Flagstaff Point with its commemorative sarsen stone. Following this are Brass Point, Rough Brow, Short Brow and Haven Brow from where

The Seven Sisters Country Park Visitor Centre.

there is a commanding view of Cuckmere Haven and the meanders of its river.

(E) Seven Sisters Country Park Visitor Centre

Here are display boards showing the animals, birds, insects and plants to be found in the park; a touch table which fascinates young and old with its skull, blocks of chalk, iron pyrites, and, until someone found it too fascinating, part of a mammoth's tooth found at Hope Gap. There is also a shop selling items of interest, a restaurant and a bike hire centre.

> The two car parks are now Pay and Display at £1 for up to three hours. Check the signs, for their gates are locked in summer at 10pm and at 5pm in winter. The Centre is open daily from the Thursday before Easter to 31 October from 10.30am to 4.30pm and to 5pm at weekends and bank holidays. In winter it is open from 11am to 4pm, weekends only.

(F) Cuckmere Haven

The Seven Sisters Country Park covers the lower part of the Cuckmere Valley and part of the Seven Sisters cliffs and is owned and managed by East Sussex County Council. There was once a little fishing village nestling near the mouth of the River Cuckmere called Exceat but repeated incursions by French raiders and the ravages of the Black Death in 1348 reduced its population by four fifths and those that were left moved away.

(G) West Dean

Alfred the Great, it is said, had a palace here but no traces of it have been so far discovered. Below the Norman church of All Saints is a pigeon tower and a massive flint wall – all that remains of the ancient manor house of the Thomas family who have a monument in the church.

(H) Charleston Manor

The Domesday survey records that: 'Ralph holds Charlston from the Count [de Mortain]'. A Tudor wing was added to the original house and a Georgian front was built between 1710-30. It stands in gardens which are sometimes open to the public.

(J) White Horse

This 90ft long figure was carved in the chalk hillside sometime in the nineteenth century, probably as a youthful prank by James Pagden, his brother and a cousin.

(K) Litlington

A pretty little village of Saxon origin, its name meaning quite simply 'Little Homestead'. It claims the distinction of having the county's first tea gardens, opened by Frederick Russell as part of the extensive pleasure grounds he created there in the 1880s. The church is Norman, with later additions, and has a weather-boarded bell tower.

> Refreshments are available at the Litlington Tea Gardens and at the Plough and Harrow pub. There is limited parking in the village.

(L) Plonk Barn

It sounds as though it ought to contain wine but it is a brick and flint building of no significance save for the fact that it marks the point where the South Downs Way footpath and bridleway meet to continue as one across the bridge into Alfriston. The barn has been modernised and is now a private house.

𝕏𝕏 𝕏𝕏 𝕏𝕏

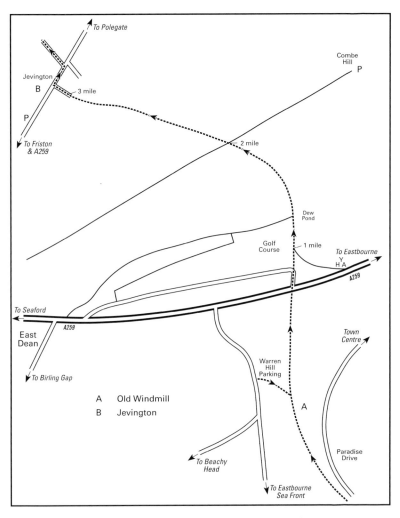

EASTBOURNE to JEVINGTON – 3 miles

Section 2

EASTBOURNE to ALFRISTON
Bridleway section – 7.5 miles (12km)

Walkers can reach the start of this section on a Route 5 or 6 Eastbourne bus from Gildredge Road, opposite Eastbourne railway station, to Meads. Alight at Carlisle Road, ascend the hill, crossing the opening of Gaudick Road and Denton Road, bear right into Paradise Drive, pass the turning into Links Road and the start of the bridleway section of the South Downs Way is on the left. Kerbside parking is permitted in Carlisle Road. Riders of horses generally start from Warren Hill car park as there is nowhere suitable to un-box at the official start.

A map board shows the route which rises through grass and bushes to Paradise Wood, past the covered-in reservoir on the right, to a point where the track divides three ways. Keep right here. Further to the right, and almost hidden in the grass, are the rough flint wall remains of an old windmill (A). From here there are extensive views over Eastbourne with Langney Point in the foreground and, beyond, the wide sweep of Pevensey Bay.

Go past the trig point on the left, where riders coming in from Warren Hill car park join the main route, which soon crosses the A259. Continue ahead along a wide track across the golf course.

At the end of the golf course the Wealdway footpath, connecting Gravesend and Beachy Head, briefly joins the South Downs Way from the right.

To reach Beachy Head Youth Hostel, tel: 01323-721081, follow the Wealdway down the scarp slope off right for 0.5mile (1km) past a maze of fire rides.

In about a mile a dew pond and dry drinking trough appear opposite a stile signposted left to East Dean. A little further on, at an ancient crosstrack, the view is magnificent. To the left is the Channel and ahead is the bull nose of Firle Beacon and below is the village of Jevington. The mass of water is the reservoir at

Arlington, with the Weald and North Downs beyond. To the right is the Iron Age hill fort at Combe Hill and, curiously sign-posted on stone plinths looking like something from a Roman villa, are Eastbourne Old Town and the villages of Willingdon and Jevington. The plinths are, in fact, part of an old Barclays

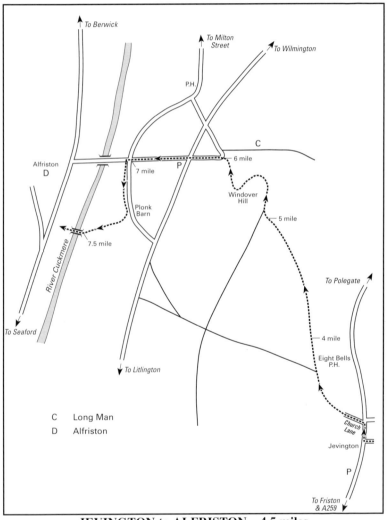

JEVINGTON to ALFRISTON – 4.5 miles

Bank which was bombed during the war, but they show the way with a certain majesty, although often obscured by high grass.

Go ahead along either track, for they soon merge into a single enclosed track on a steady descent into Jevington **(B)**.

Hawthorne Lodge tea gardens are on the right where the Way joins the road, with Jiggs Cottage B&B on the left.

There is a car park 50 yards to the left from this junction.

Turn right for 50 yards, then left up Church Lane, opposite the Hungry Monk restaurant and past the church of St Andrews. This is a delightful section of the Way with paddocks on either side. Keep ahead, rising all the way, taking great care in a wooded section where there are a lot of exposed roots underfoot.

At a clearing turn right in the direction of a SDW signpost. Pass through a gate and along a well-defined path across open downland with the remains of Hill Barn clearly visible to the right and a full water trough left.

Continue round the head of Deep Dean, with the White Horse (see page 19), on the side of High and Over hill opposite. Pass through a gate before bearing left round Windover Hill along a chalky track with Arlington Reservoir straight ahead and Alfriston down to the left. At the staggered cross tracks the Way keeps left.

To visit the Long Man of Wilmington **(C)** take the right fork, keeping alongside the fence on the right until you come to a gate. Go through the gate and the path leads to the foot of the Long Man.

The descent to Alfriston passes below Windover reservoir then through a gate to cross the Litlington to Wilmington road – there is parking available here – keeping ahead as far as the metalled road at a triangular junction.

Bear left through a gate in the direction of the SDW signpost keeping alongside the fence on the left as far as the bridge opposite Plonk Barn, where turn right across the River Cuckmere into Alfriston **(D)**.

POINTS OF INTEREST

(A) Windmill
There was a mill here in 1724 and a little to the north stood an

earlier post mill. The remains of the flint walls are approximately 50 feet (15m) in diameter and within them is the excavated rectangular base of a bolting house.

(B) Jevington

Jevington is of Saxon origin. It is particulary attractive around the Church of St Andrew, which dates back to the early tenth century. The tapsell gate in the churchyard is unique, for not only does it swing on a central axis but it also has a stile incorporated in it. Some tombs in the graveyard were used by smugglers to hide their contraband in the eighteenth century and it was not unknown for the parson to be actively involved in their activities.

> Refreshments available at the Eight Bells public house. Car park in the village. Jiggs Cottage B&B Tel: 01323-482505.

(C) The Long Man

The largest chalk figure in England, The Long Man is as much a mystery today as he ever has been. The figure is 235ft high and preserved with white painted concrete blocks. It was first recorded in 1710 but its origin is unknown. It could be prehistoric, Saxon, Roman or made by monks from nearby Wilmington Priory in the early Middle Ages.

> Best viewed from the Priory car park, where there are toilets. Refreshments available at the Giants Rest inn at the A27 end of the village.

(D) Alfriston

Once a Saxon settlement, this lovely downland village is known as the Capital of the Downs. Its fine square boasts a spreading chestnut tree and a much-restored fifteenth century market cross, rivalled in the county only by a much grander example in Chichester.

Buildings either side of the High Street display all the main characteristic materials of the area – timber frames filled with daub and plaster or covered by weather-boarding or rich, red tiles. Houses, tearooms, shops and restaurants jostle for position along with four inns of character, the most renowned being the Star Inn which has been everything in its time from a resting place for pilgrims to a haunt for smugglers.

Waterloo Square, Alfriston with its chestnut tree and market cross.

The Old Clergy House was the first property bought by the National Trust for £10 in 1896. It stands on the edge of the Tye, an old Saxon name for a village green, which is dominated by the church of St Andrews, known because of its size as the Cathedral of the Downs. It was built about 1360 and has no later additions.

ACCOMMODATION:

The YHA is about a mile south of Alfriston and can be reached by taking the roadside footpath or the riverside footpath to Frog Firle. Tel: 01323-870423

B&B is available at:

Meadowbank,	Riverdale House,	Russets,
Sloe Lane,	Seaford Road,	Deans Road,
Alfriston BN26 5UR	Alfriston BN26 5TR.	Alfriston BN26 5XJ
Tel: 01323-870742	Tel: 01323-871038	Tel: 01323-870626

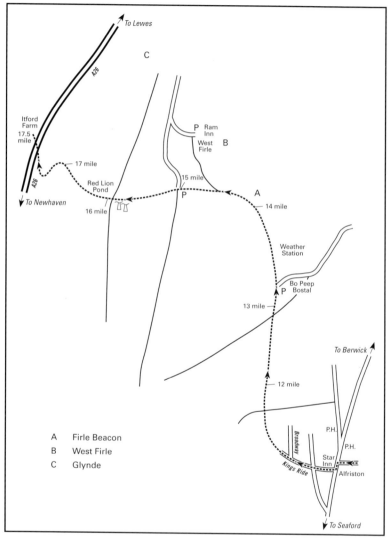

ALFRISTON to ITFORD FARM – 6.5 miles.

Section 3

ALFRISTON to RODMELL
8.2 miles (13.3km)

Leave Alfriston to the left of the Star Inn. Go straight ahead at the crossroads into Kings Ride, keeping ahead along the chalky track as the metalled road swings off right into the Broadway.

Follow the track as it climbs, ignoring all side tracks, and keep ahead in the direction of the SDW marker post as the main track turns off left, and ahead again in 20 yards at the cross-tracks. Now the Way cuts across open Downland as far as a kissing gate beside a bridle gate – why two gates where one would do is a mystery. Continue alongside the fence on the left. Here there are good views across the Weald, Arlington Reservoir and the distant North Downs to the right.

As the fence turns away to the left, keep ahead along an obvious route descending to Bo Peep Bostal car park behind which is a picnic site with three seats offering splendid views over the Weald.

Pass through two sets of gates into the Firle Estate with its enclosed weather station on the right as the gradual climb to the top of Firle Beacon (**A**) begins.

The Way is almost level from the Beacon to the car park at the head of Firle Bostal, a metalled road taking much traffic from the village of West Firle (**B**) below.

A water trough stands just before the gate leading to a broad green sward cut across the Downs to the car park, beyond which is the square outline of a reservoir and the twin radio masts beckoning from the top of Beddingham Hill. There are brief glimpses of Mount Caburn and Glynde (**C**) over to the right and to the left is Newhaven and the sea.

Join a gravel track past the masts and follow a fairly desolate stretch as far as the trig point beside Red Lion pond, a dried out dew pond. Now Piddinghoe Pond can be seen to the left with its little island and the boats of its sailing club perhaps skimming the water or moored ashore.

From the top of Itford Hill the whole of the Ouse valley comes into view with the villages of Southease, Iford, Northease and Rodmell on the far side of the river.

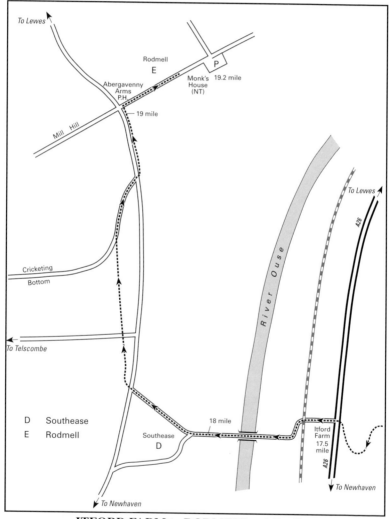

ITFORD FARM to RODMELL – 1.7 miles.

The Way descends round left then, at a waymarker, turns back right along a deep farm track as far as the bridle gate. Then on to the busy A26 which has to be crossed with care into Itford Farm, where there is a water point and a horse trough. Continue through the farm and over the railway at Southease station to cross the River Ouse by the swing bridge which used to be opened to allow boats to pass upstream to Lewes. Redshank and oystercatcher are a common sight hereabouts and cormorants and herons are often seen in the adjacent drainage ditches.

Carry on into Southease (**D**) as far as the Lewes-Newhaven road, which cross and turn right. Cross the road leading to Telscombe, then through the gate, bearing right in the direction of the SDW waymarker, through a thicket and another gate to turn left into Cricketing Bottom.

To reach Rodmell (**E**) turn right here as far as the road and cross into the village. Monk's House and car park are about 500 yards down The Street.

POINTS OF INTEREST

(A) Firle Beacon

At 713ft (217m) Firle Beacon is one of the highest points on the Downs and it also marks the change of direction from west-east to south-east. On top of the Beacon – the site of one of a line of warning beacon fires at the time of the Spanish Armada – is a huge barrow which, according to legend, housed the remains of a giant in a silver coffin. In common with other burial mounds in the area its contents, if any, were probably removed by Victorian antiquarians.

(B) West Firle

A look at the map will not reveal an East Firle, nor a north or a south one either, and the village is always referred to as Firle. There was, however, once a village east of here known as Heighton St Clare. When Eleanor St Clare married John Gage of Cirencester in the early 1400s she brought her estates with her and these were augmented by the marriage of their son, William, to Agnes Bolney, co-heiress of the manor of Firle, in 1472 and the Gage family have lived here ever since. Firle Place is regularly open to the public and contains a magnificent collection of furniture and works of art.

Refreshments at the Ram Inn. The Dairy Farmhouse, Wick Street, Firle, offers B&B. Tel: 01273-858280.

(C) Glynde

The magnificent Elizabethen mansion, Glynde Place, was built in 1567 and a subsequent owner, Richard Trevor, Bishop of Durham, redesigned its interior on classic Georgian lines. He also built Glynde church, which is a miniature version of St Paul's cathedral in flint. Glyndebourne, which has been in the same family for seven centuries, is older and the original opera house was added in 1934. A new one was built in 1994.

(D) Southease

The simple church with its Norman round tower replaces the Saxon one mentioned in a charter of 966, and looks down on to the rambling village green. Inside is a Jacobean chancel arch of wood, lath and plaster and reproductions of some early medieval wall paintings, the originals of which have almost totally faded away. This village had a flourishing fishery at the time of the Domesday survey when it was assessed for 38,500 herrings and '£4 for porpoises'.

Southease church.

(E) Rodmell

Here there is another Norman church, this one approached through the school playground. Inside is a memorial brass to the de la Chambre family who owned the long-gone mansion, Rodmell Place, in the fifteenth and sixteenth centuries. The most renowned building in the village today is, of course, Monk's House, bought in 1919 by Leonard and Virginia Woolf for £700 and now a place of pilgrimage for Bloomsbury Group devotees from all over the world.

The Woolfs spent their time between here and London until 1940 when their town house was bombed. The following year Virginia drowned herself in the Ouse and her ashes are buried in the garden of Monk's House. Leonard remained here until his death in 1969 when the house became the property of the National Trust.

Refreshments at the Abergavenny Arms.

Mrs Pauline Cherry, 1 Sunnyside Cottages, Rodmell BN7 3HA. Tel: 01273-476876 offers B&B.

ACCOMMODATION IN TELSCOMBE

The YHA, tel: 01273-301357, is in the village by the church. To visit Telscombe turn left along Cricketing Bottom, instead of right for Rodmell, and continue past the farm buildings for a further mile.

B&B also available at:
Stud Farm House, Telscombe Village. Tel: 01273-302486
Camping, stabling and grazing.

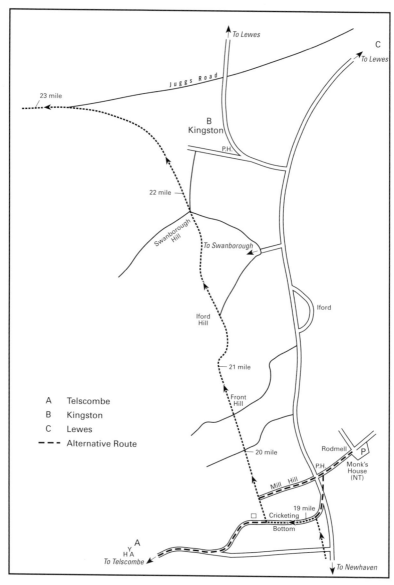

RODMELL to JUGGS ROAD – 4.8 miles

Section 4

RODMELL to PYECOMBE
13.8miles (22.2km)

Return to the Way along Cricketing Bottom, turning right just short of the farm buildings, soon to bear right again through a gate and up a slope to continue alongside a fence on the right for a short stretch before continuing ahead towards the large house.

> To visit Telscombe (**A**) continue for one mile (1.6km) past the farm buildings and return. Alternatively leave Rodmell across the crossroads by the forge, proceeding along Mill Lane which was the old SDW route, to rejoin the new route at Mill Hill.

Continue down the narrow path to the right of Mill Hill, through an enclosed stretch with trees and high hedges on either side soon to lead to a gate where the Way opens out with magnificent views across the Ouse valley to Mount Caburn.

The Way crosses two farm tracks before keeping ahead along a long section of concrete track up Iford Hill. There are good views back from here over Newhaven, Seaford Head and the start of the Seven Sisters.

As the concrete track swings off left towards a barn on the skyline, the SDW turns sharp right and in about 50 yards left through a gate. Keep alongside the fence on the left as the route skirts the top of Swanborough Hill.

Where the Way follows the fence round left there are good views of Kingston-near-Lewes down to the right with a tiny memorial stone to E.G. 26.12.59 by the fence.

> This stone commemorates Mrs Greenwood, the mother of a local farmer.

When the track turns off left over a cattle grid another chalky track leads off right down to Swanborough. About 20 yards down this track another track leads off left in the direction of Kingston church (**B**). The SDW continues ahead at this crossing, through a gate and along an obvious path past the Dew Pond Project on the right, a recent restoration by Northease School in conjunction with the South Downs Rangers. A little further on,

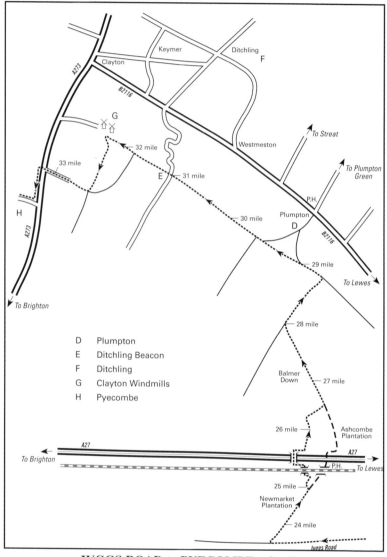

D   Plumpton
E   Ditchling Beacon
F   Ditchling
G   Clayton Windmills
H   Pyecombe

JUGGS ROAD to PYECOMBE – 9 miles.

as the Way begins to swing to the left, it passes a dried out dew pond which has been replaced by a trough fed by a portable water carrier. Continue over a stile – or go through the gate – keeping alongside the fence on the right. This is Juggs Road, the old route taken by the Brighton fishwives on their way over the hills to sell their produce in Lewes. They carried their wares in pottery jugs – hence the name of this byway.

To visit Lewes (**C**) turn right here, following Juggs Road with the fence on the left on its straight route into the county town.

Pass a gas pressure reducing station before crossing a stile or passing through a metal gate, turning off right in the direction of the SDW waymarker towards the storm-damaged beeches of Newmarket Plantation.

Continue downhill, turning left at the fingerpost through a gate to follow an obvious route under the railway bridge and along a metalled road. Turn right over the bridge across the busy A27 before turning right again past Housedean Farm. Turn left at the fingerpost up a series of wide steps, then through a gate and continue along the edge of the next field before entering the woods along an earthy track. Turn left through a gate beside a style, following the familiar flint and chalk track ahead, the ridges of a Celtic field system barely visible now to the left as it steadily climbs Balmer Down.

Pass underneath the electricity powerlines before turning right at the T-junction where there are good views over old Lewes racecourse to the right. Soon the Way takes a sharp turn to the left as a gate appears to bar the way ahead.

Through the gate is a route over Blackcap and Mount Harry before skirting the converted buildings of the old racecourse to Lewes. A path to the left off this route descends steeply to Plumpton (**D**). Both routes are well signposted.

The views to the right along this next section looking across the Weald are particularly spectacular as the Way descends gently past Streathill Farm on its way to Ditchling Beacon (**E**) where there is usually the welcome sight of an ice cream vendor. It is possible from here to descend into Ditchling (**F**) although at 227m it is quite a climb back.

From the Beacon the Way descends gently to a gate, beyond which is a new memorial Keymer Post on the right. The old divide between East and West Sussex is 100 yards further on. Beyond this the route passes through another gate, this one beside a metal gate, then keeps ahead towards the sails of Jack and Jill, the Clayton windmills **(G)**.

About 100 yards before the windmills the Way turns left, past the stables, before turning right at the cross-tracks with Pyecombe golf course on the left.

Cross the A273, turning left along a sandy path before turning right along School Lane into Pyecombe **(H)**.

POINTS OF INTEREST

(A) Telscombe

Ambrose Gorham is responsible for this little piece of unspoiled England. A retired bookmaker turned racehorse owner, he became squire and benefactor of Telscombe at the end of the nineteenth century and refused to permit any development but he did improve the living conditions of the inhabitants. It was the first village in Sussex to have electricity and had mains

Telscombe village hall.

water in 1909. When Squire Gorham died in 1933 he left all his land to Brighton Corporation in trust, stating in his will that the purpose of the gift was to preserve the rural nature of the village. The trust still exists and Telscombe has retained its tranquility and individuality.

(B) Kingston-near-Lewes

The thirteenth century Church of St Pancras with its unusual tapsell gate swinging on its central axis is the first building of note in a lane of flint cottages.

> The Juggs Arms at the end of the lane offers refreshments. B&B at Nightingales, The Avenue, Kingston, BN7 3L, tel: 01273-475673 and at Settlands, Wellgreen Lane, Kingston, tel: 01273-472295. Camping at Spring Barn Farm, tel: 01273-472528.

(C) Lewes

The county town and administrative centre for East Sussex, Lewes has probably more history than anywhere else in the county. Evidence of prehistoric occupation has been found in the area. It was here, on 16 May 1246 after the defeat of Henry III by Simon de Montfort and the barons, that the Mise of Lewes was signed and the seeds of parliamentary democracy were sown.

> Information on points of interest is available from the Tourist Information Centre, 187 High Street, Lewes BN7 2DE, tel: 01273-483448

The Battle of Lewes commemorative sculpture in the Priory grounds.

(D) Plumpton

Opposite the Agricultural College is the half-timbered Tudor splendour of Plumpton Place where, in the sixteenth century, botanist Leonard Mascall developed the first pippin apple and is said to have introduced the carp to England.

Looking across the green to the church at Ditchling.

(E) Ditchling Beacon

At 227m (750 feet) this is the second highest point on the South Downs. There is still evidence of an Iron Age hill fort on the steep northern slope although most of it has been damaged by modern farming and erosion. As the name suggests the hill was one of a chain of beacon fires warning of the Spanish Armada. On a clear day there are extensive views across the Weald for 30 miles or more.

(F) Ditchling

The manor of Ditchling was once the property of King Alfred and later belonged to Edward the Confessor. Edward II kept a stud of horses here and in 1312 granted a charter for a weekly market. It has some lovely timbered cottages and opposite the church is the ornately-timbered Wings Place. The old church school has been converted into a museum housing, among other fascinating local artefacts, relics of triple murderer, Jacob Harris, whose decomposing body hung for years on a gibbet on the common.

(G) Clayton windmills

Jack is a brick tower mill and Jill is a white painted post mill. Jill, the older of the two, was built in Brighton in 1821 and later moved to its present site. Jack was built in 1866 and both mills worked until 1908. In 1973 Jack was restored by Universal Pictures for a location sequence in the film *The Black Windmill*. There is now a Jack and Jill Preservation Society, for it is important that both mills survive as they are such good examples of two distinct types – the brick built tower mill and the older wooden post mill.

(H) Pyecombe

A distinctive type of shepherd's crook with a curled end was produced here in the nineteenth century. The gate latch to the church is even made out of the curved iron top of a crook that was actually produced in the building opposite, for the single-storey extension to the house was once a forge. Today it is a tea room but most of the original forge has been preserved.

Refreshments at the Plough Inn.

A regular bus service operates from Pyecombe to Brighton, passing the YHA in Patcham. Tel: 01273-556196.

For accommodation in Brighton:
The Tourist Information Centre, 10 Bartholomew Square, Brighton, BN1 1JS. Tel: 01273-323755

Section 5

PYECOMBE to WASHINGTON
14miles (22.5km)

From the church cross the bridge over the busy A23 turning left past Brendon Riding School before turning up right along a surfaced lane. Continue through a metal gate and past a water trough before starting the climb up a broad chalk path to the top of West Hill from where the view looking back is tremendous.

Pass through a gate beside a fingerpost and down a field of thick pasture to another gate leading into a narrow, wooded track which may well be muddy in wet weather.

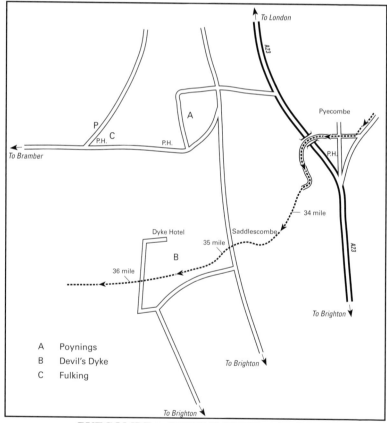

PYECOMBE to DEVIL'S DYKE – 4 miles

Keep to the right of the barbed wire fence with the farm on the left and the cottages which form the tiny hamlet of Saddlescombe to the right. Once past the farm buildings turn down left in the direction of a marker post, through a gate to the road which cross to continue along a path to the left.

The road to the right leads to Poynings (**A**), about half a mile away.

Pass the corner of a raised reservoir with its iron railing fence to carry on along the main track ignoring all paths off left. The deep dry valley of Devil's Dyke (**B**) is visible to the right but keep ahead until it joins a bridle-path coming in from the left. Continue ahead to the road.

Turn right at the road across the head of the Dyke to visit the Dyke Hotel where there is a large car park and refreshments available.

The Way continues across the road in the direction of the masts on Truleigh Hill. Past the fingerpost in the middle of the next field the route is evident to a bridle gate. Take the right fork once through the gate along a wide, chalky track which undulates across a wide expanse of the Downs.

In about half a mile (0.8km) where an obvious track merges in from the left opposite the raised mound of an old Iron Age tumulus, a fingerpost points sharp right downhill along a sunken track between high banks. About half way down the side of the hill another fingerpost to the left points to Fulking (**C**).

The main route heads across Fulking Hill, from where there are glimpses of Edburton church down to the right, then it dips sharply before heading up Edburton Hill and the even higher Truleigh Hill with its distinctive communication masts (**D**).

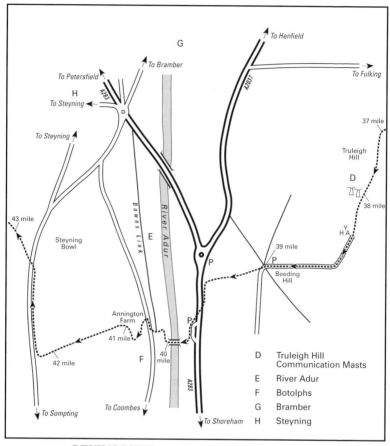

DEVIL'S DYKE to STEYNING BOWL – 6 miles.

Over the brow of the next hill the Way passes Truleigh Hill YHA Hostel, tel: 01903-813419, with its water point and catering facilities. It was built in the 1930s as a summer house and has been extended and modernised to become one of the association's finest hostels.

Just beyond here the track becomes a metalled road offering a speedy section for cyclists although a bridleway running parallel to the Way on the right provides easier going on foot and for horses. The views across the Weald to the right along this stretch are really quite splendid.

In about a mile (1.6km) at the car park below Beeding Hill is a six-way path junction where the metalled road takes a left turn and the Way keeps straight ahead through a bridle gate and into a field. The River Adur comes into view ahead with the Gothic spires of Lancing College visible to the left. Through another gate before making a gradual descent alongside the deep valley of Anchor Bottom on the left to the A283 Shoreham to Steyning road.

Turn left here, crossing the road with care into the lay-by opposite. About half way along cut through right along a sandy path to the bridge taking the Way across the Adur **(E)**.

There is a tap and drinking trough for horses here erected in 1985 by the Society of Sussex Downsmen.

Follow the riverbank for about 200 yards when the Way turns away from the river towards the tiny hamlet of Botolphs **(F)**.

To visit Bramber **(G)** either keep to the riverbank or turn right along the newly constructed Downs Link path, following the distinctive sandy path into the village.

Turn left at the road to visit the church while the Way continues right through Annington Farm and as far as a fingerpost pointing off left where it leaves the metalled road to continue along a broad farm drive as far as the turn off left to Tinpotts Cottage. Veer right here following the fence on the left to the end of an extensive field where there is a gate and a signpost pointing right. Follow the fence on the right now as it turns left alongside Bramber Beeches, a group of trees planted by the West Sussex Federation of Women's Institutes to commemorate their Diamond Jubilee in 1979.

Follow the fence as far as the road where turn right keeping to the right of the road past the hang glider's car park. Where the road bears right cross over and go through a gate where a SDW signpost indicates the route which passes the memorial stone to Walter Langmead, a Sussex farmer. Continue ahead bearing round left past the trig point on the left.

At this multiple junction a track leading off right drops down into Steyning **(H)**, about two miles away..

The ramparts of Cissbury Ring hill fort are visible from here and Chanctonbury Ring **(J)** gets ever nearer. The Way curves gently to the left of this famous clump of beech trees from where

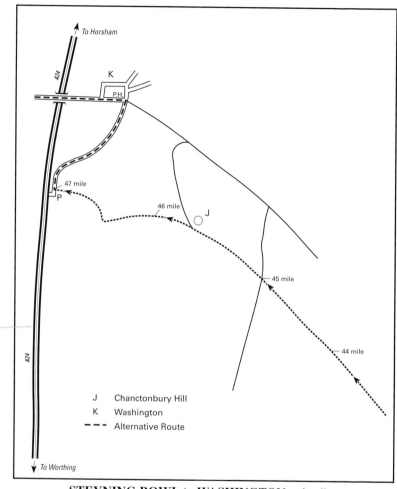

STEYNING BOWL to WASHINGTON – 4 miles

there are magnificent views in all directions. Pass the trig point and dew pond before continuing along an obvious chalk path for only a short distance before a fingerpost indicates the Way goes to the right along a rough track beside a hedge.

Once the track begins its descent, passing a gas pressure-reducing station on the right, the busy A24 comes into view with Washington away to the right. At the bottom of the hill is a car park with tourist information point and the Way turns left onto the approach road which soon joins the loop road to Washington **(K)**.

> To visit the village turn right onto the loop road following it half a mile or so. The main route continues left to cross the A24 although there is a safer alternative route from Washington. Both routes are described in Section 6.

POINTS OF INTEREST

(A) Poynings

The fourteenth century Church of the Holy Trinity was built under the will of Michael de Poynygges, Lord of the Manor, who died in 1369 and from whom the village takes its name. George Beard was probably rector for the longest period, fifty-four years in the eighteenth century, although it is said he used only two texts for his sermons throughout his entire incumbency. Those who succeeded him found a very neglected church and from the beginning of the nineteenth century much restoration work was carried out.

> Refreshments at the Royal Oak public house.

> B&B at Dyke Lane Cottage, Dyke Lane, Poynings. Tel: 01273-857335

(B) Devil's Dyke

Although attributed to the Devil this curved valley almost a mile long (1.6km) and 700 feet high (215m) is most likely a coombe formed at the end of the Ice Age. The promontory between the Dyke and the escarpment made it an obvious choice for an Iron Age hill fort, ramparts of which are still clearly visible, and there are magnificent views from the car park. This has been a popular tourist attraction for more than 200 years and the first hotel was built here in 1817. A subsequent proprietor boosted its popularity even further by building a railway up the side of the Downs.

> Refreshments at the Dyke Hotel.

The South Downs Way approaching the bridge across the Adur.

A waymarker points to Chanctonbury Ring.

(C) Fulking

A pretty little village with paint-washed cottages yet unusually without a church. At the beginning of the nineteenth century sheep outnumbered humans ten to one and neighbouring downland farmers sent their flocks to its sheepwash before the annual shearing. The spring gushes out of the hillside just by the Shepherd and Dog pub and the stream it feeds was dammed to form a sheepwash at the bend in the lane.

(D) Truleigh Hill Communication Masts

The first mast, which was here in 1940, was one of a chain of masts along the South Coast which was part of Britain's secret radar defence system.

(E) River Adur

Michael Drayton gave the river this name in *Polyolbion,* his top-ographical guide to England published in 1622, in the mistaken belief that the Roman harbour of *Portus Adurni* (Portsmouth) was at its mouth. Before that it was known as Bramber Water after the medieval port of Bramber on its west bank.

(F) Botolphs

The church in this hamlet is recorded as St Botolph's in 1288. The present Norman church was built on the Saxon foundations of a church known as St Peter's-by-the-Bridge for there was, it is believed, a bridge nearby carrying the Roman Cornwall to Anderida tin trade route across the Adur river.

(G) Bramber

Little more than one massive wall remains of the Norman castle built by William de Braose in 1083 although the church adjoining it is of the same period and has survived virtually intact. St Mary's, a fine example of a medieval timber-framed house, is further into the village and is open to the public.

Refreshments and B&B at the Castle Hotel. Tel: 01903-812102

(H) Steyning

A delightful place with many old buildings, among them the Old Market House with its clock tower which dominates the High Street, an old grammar school and a church so fine to be almost of cathedral quality. It is on the site of the one founded by St Cuthman in the eighth century when the Adur was much

Chanctonbury Ring, its beeches still showing the ravages of the October 1987 storm.

wider and Steyning an important port. According to legend St Cuthman was wheeling his old mother in a wheelbarrow from Devon to a destination unknown when it broke down at Steyning. He took this as a sign to settle and built a hut for his mother and himself and a wooden church for the inhabitants.

(J) Chanctonbury Ring

This famous clump of beech trees, decimated in the 1987 hurricane, was planted in 1760 by the young Charles Goring of Wiston House. It is said he climbed the hill daily with bottles of water to aid their early progress and he lived to see them grow into maturity for he was ninety when he died. The landmark is visible from a distance of more than 60km away and in the centre of the ring is the site of a square Romano-Celtic temple in which coins and pottery were found dating back to 100AD.

(K) Washington

It was here, at Chanctonbury Farm, that a great find of Saxon coins was made in 1866, consisting of an urn containing some 3,000 pennies from the reigns of Edward the Confessor and

Harold II. When the Treasury eventually got hold of those that had not been sold locally, they were found to have come from some fifty different mints, including those at Hastings, Lewes, Steyning and Chichester.

Charles Goring is buried in the churchyard from which his famous clump of beech trees can be seen. However, his grave is behind the church, which blocks any view of the Ring.

Refreshments available at the Frankland Arms

Washington Caravan and Camping Park, London Road, Washington, West Sussex RH20 4HA. Tel: 01903-892869

Buses go north to Storrington, Pulborough and Horsham, and south to Worthing from Washington.

Section 6

WASHINGTON to AMBERLEY
6.25 miles (10.1km)

Two routes begin this section; the first route continues across the
A24 and the second route takes a detour through the village of
Washington. Both routes meet up within two miles to continue
the section into Amberley.

Route 1 crosses the A24 to continue into Glaseby Lane which
climbs steeply alongside the dual carriageway before turning
sharp left where there is a water point available. Near the top of
the hill the metalled surface gives way to rough gravel with a
fence on the right and open arable land to the left. Down
beyond the fence are the trees of Biggen Holt and looking back
still further the square tower of Washington church.

The track goes on over the summit of Barnsfarm Hill and
within a mile of leaving the A24 reaches a fingerpost pointing

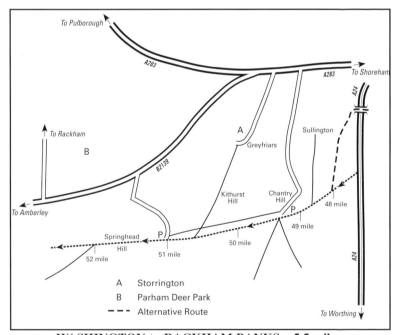

WASHINGTON to RACKHAM BANKS – 5.5 miles.

right which indicates the alternative route of the SDW where the two routes meet.

Route 2 starts from the village along The Street which gives direct access to the church on the right. Beyond the church the Way crosses a modern bridge over the A24 continuing to a point where the metalled road keeps straight ahead and the right-of-way forks right to Rowdell House, a lovely old building built of stone. In front of the house turn left into a short green lane then through a gate (or between the posts) to rejoin the metalled road which follow up the hill. As it bends right into the woods pass through a gate to follow a hedged grassy track to another gate. The Way is an obvious route from here through arable fields and up to the fingerpost where turn right to rejoin the alternative route of the SDW.

Head towards the barn where the chalk path noticeably gives way to sandstone. A track off right leads to Sullington, with its attractive chantry and delightful little church, and there are wide panoramas of the Weald at this point.

The small car park is at Chantry Post with tracks leading off in five directions. The arms of the signpost are all missing, so it is not much use but the road comes up from Storrington and the SDW keeps straight ahead.

The larger car park at Kithurst Hill is much more popular and there is a pleasant track off right leading through the woods own to Greyfriars Farm at the head of Greyfriars Lane into Storrington **(A)**.

From the car park the Way climbs gently along a broad track to the summit of Springhead Hill where there is a small wood. Just beyond here take the right fork where the track is fenced on either side. There are glorious views right over the Weald and soon of Parham Deer Park **(B)** with its large house, woods, ponds and follies.

The trig point on the left atop Rackham Hill, which is more than 600ft above sea level, is reached without a great sense of climbing and just beyond are Rackham Banks, a substantial if little known earthwork.

The Way begins to descend slightly now over Amberley

Mount to reach a stile by a gate from where the view is breath-taking.

The drop down past Downs Farm is quite steep with a fence on the right. Through another gate by a stile, descending still further as the path becomes much narrower – so cyclists and riders do take care here.

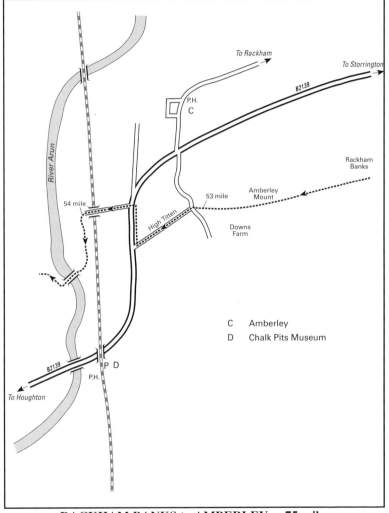

RACKHAM BANKS to AMBERLEY – .75 miles

Descend to the metalled road where turn right, taking the left fork down High Titten.

The right fork leads to the village of Amberley (**C**).

The main route turns right at the B2139. To visit the Chalk Pits Museum (**D**) turn left, following the main road to the railway station, taking care for there is no pavement.

POINTS OF INTEREST

(A) Storrington

A small bustling town with a restored church with columns of the nave dating from the fifteenth century.

Inside is a brass of Henry Wilsha who died in 1591 after being rector for forty years. The reredos has scenes from the life of Christ with figures carved in stone. The elaborately-carved door in the wall of Abbey House, opposite the church, was made by an Eastern craftsman who copied, in Indian mahogany, the famous

The Abbey House door.

doors at Lahore. It is made up of hundreds of carved pieces depicting birds, fishes and many tiny medallions.

Refreshments are available at a choice of venue. Luxury B&B is offered by Mrs Walton, 1 Lime Close, Storrington, RH20 4LX. Tel: 01903-740437.

(B) Parham Deer Park

The 500 acre park is full of a rich variety of trees, shrubs and

Amberley village.

bushes with lily ponds, deer and herons. The church across the lawn has one of only three lead fonts in Sussex and the oldest of its kind in all England. The house, in which is displayed a fine collection of furniture, portraits and needlework, and the park, are open to the public.

(C) Amberley

A village of tiny cottages of flint and timber and substantial stone farmhouses. Until the 1960s it was the centre for the production of lime, which was dug out of the chalk hills to the south of the village. Its castle is a fortified manor, at one time the country residence of the Bishops of Chichester. The River Arun, to the west of the village, is tidal and high tides coupled with heavy rain used to cause the water meadows known as the Wildbrooks to flood. This problem has been rectified by raising the embankments to their present level.

Refreshments available at the Black Horse and the Bridge Inn.

B&B at: Bacons, Amberley BN18 9NY. Tel: 01798-831234

Bus services from Amberley are infrequent but there is a regular rail link with London and to Arundel and Portsmouth.

Looking down from the South Downs Way on to Amberley's Chalk Pits Museum and some of its exhibits.

(D) Chalk Pits Museum

The old chalk pits have been turned into an open-air museum depicting rural industries with working exhibits covering a wide variety of trades including those of a brickmaker, blacksmith and wheelwright. An industrial railway exhibition has some thirty locomotives in a variety of narrow gauges and there is a great bank of kilns in which the chalk was burnt.

Open March to October, Wednesday to Sunday, and Bank Holiday Mondays from 10am to 5pm. Open daily during school holidays.

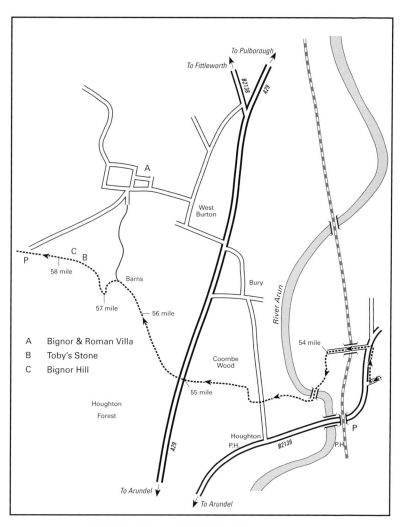

AMBERLEY to BIGNOR HILL – 4.5 miles

Section 7

AMBERLEY to COCKING
11.5 miles (18.5km)

At the bottom of High Titten turn right along the path adjacent to the B2139. The signpost on this corner is roughly the half way stage of the South Downs Way – Eastbourne 50 miles to the east, Winchester 51 miles westward.

Cross the road at the obvious point, continuing ahead as far as the concrete road by New Barn, where turn left over the railway and past a small sewerage treatment works on the left.

Follow the Way round left, through a gate to turn right along the river embankment as far as the bridge. Cross the River Arun here, turning right along the opposite bank before turning off left at the bend in the river.

The Way works its route round to the right, then the left, before crossing the road and continuing ahead along a wide chalky track between two fields. Looking back there are good views of Amberley Mount, appearing far more formidable from this point with the steep descent past Downs Farm clearly visible.

As the track begins its climb towards Coombe Wood there are good views of the Arun as it meanders through the water meadows of the Wildbrooks with the little church of Bury coming into view. It is a steep climb past the edge of Coombe Wood to the busy A29, which cross and turn right for about 50 yards before turning left at a familiar signpost seemingly indicating all the past effort was to cover just one mile.

The Way begins to level out now and soon comes to a junction where keep to the main track as it swings up right at the rather confusing crosstracks signpost.

Avoid the track leading off left at all costs for it goes into the deep, dark Houghton Forest.

Another signpost by a row of bushes in about 100 yards confirms the route, with a field now between the Way and the forest. The twin radio masts between Sutton Down and Bignor Hill are clearly visible now and the track can be seen winding its way ahead round Bignor Hill towards them.

Pass three barns, where the obvious route for the Way seems to continue ahead – but this track leads down to Bignor and Bignor Roman Villa (**A**).

Instead, make a sudden zigzag left, then right, to follow the

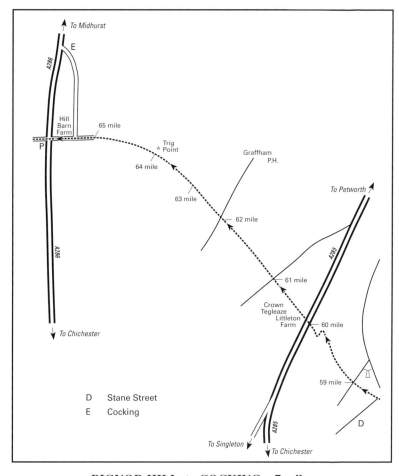

BIGNOR HILL to COCKING – 7 miles

track as it swings left on its climb up Bignor Hill, turning right as it merges with a much wider track on the rest of the ascent to Toby's Stone **(B)**.

The summit of Bignor Hill **(C)** is quickly reached now and the National Trust car park can be seen at the end of a long, straight stretch.

The track continues ahead towards the twin masts but the Way turns left onto Stane Street **(D)**, following the fence on the right as it runs alongside a piece of Roman history for 150 yards or so before veering off right as far as a gate.

Continue alongside a fence on the left across a huge field keeping ahead at the crosstracks on leaving the Slindon Estate. The track becomes smooth chalk as it skirts above Scotcher's Bottom with little of interest to see on either side, then it runs into woodland and soon

Signpost on Bignor Hill with the Way passing to the right.

the buildings of Littleton Farm on the A285 come into view.

As the Way begins to descend more steeply the track does a zig-zag left, then right, along a dry, chalky track which can become lethal in wet weather. Fortunately there is a raised walkway to the right as far as the road.

Cross the A285 and turn right, turning left in 20 yards to bear right up the drive by the telegraph pole. Pass through two gates in quick succession into a field, keeping in the direction of the SDW signpost. The way ahead is obvious across the first field but may be less evident across the second as this is one of the few fields along the South Downs Way that is ploughed up from time to time. If the climb up through both fields seemed onerous then little wonder for Crown Tegleaze to the left is the highest point on the South Downs at 830ft (253m). However, the view looking back on reaching the gate into the woods makes the effort worthwhile.

A short section through woodland emerges at the Tegleaze crosstracks where there is a signpost erected by the Cowdray Hunt. The views ahead and to the right are stunning and the Way continues along a chalk and gravel track as far as the oak signpost at Graffham Down, erected by the Society of Sussex Downsmen to commemorate Sir Edmond Barkworth, one of their more dynamic members.

A track off to the right here leads down to Graffham church and village about 3km away with a choice of accommodation. Upper Norwood Farm, Graffham, Petworth, GU28 0QG offers B&B, stabling and grazing Tel: 01798-867264 and there is the Camping and Caravan Club Site, Great Bury, Graffham, Petworth, GU28 0QJ Tel: 01798-867476

The White Horse pub offers a warm welcome to walkers.

From here the Way enters dense woodland for more than two miles (3.2km) and becomes stony underfoot. With the lack of views it is difficult to imagine the track runs along such high ground and it is only on reaching a clearing when the track twists left then right that the going becomes smooth again.

A trig point is in a field to the right and a little further on there is a raised 'hide', now neglected, which was once part of the Cowdray Estate's deer shooting project that happily seems to have been abandoned.

It is a pleasant drop down to Hill Barn Farm with a splendid vista ahead and the Way clearly visible climbing over Cocking Down.

There is a water tap at Hill Barn Farm and a footpath leading off opposite to Cocking village (**E**) half a mile away.

Continue down Hillbarn Lane to the A286 where there is a car park and adjacent bus stop with buses to Midhurst, Singleton and Chichester.

The fifteenth century Ivy Cottage, formerly the village shop at Bignor.

POINTS OF INTEREST

(A) Bignor and Roman Villa

This is definitely a detour worth taking. Not only is the village attractive but it has a fifteenth century cottage which became the village shop and has featured on many calendars. But it is the Roman Villa that is the major interest here for it is one of the largest of its kind in England, covering four or five acres. It has more than sixty compartments, some in a splendid state of preservation, with mosaics displaying the fine craftmanship of the Roman era. One room has its hypocaust revealed to show how a Roman central heating system worked all those centuries ago.

Open March to October daily (except Monday) 10am to 5pm and 10am to 6pm during the summer months.

(B) Toby's Stone

This is a monument in the form of a large mounting block to the memory of James Wentworth Fitzwilliam-Toby, a former secretary of the Cowdray Hunt, who died in 1955. On the reverse of the stone, which was virtually destroyed by vandals in 1999, was a memorial to his wife Beryl, who died in 1960.

(C) Bignor Hill

Belongs to the National Trust as part of the 1,400 hectare Slindon estate bequeathed by Mr J F Wootton Isaacson in 1950. At 750 ft (225m) it is one of the highest summits on the South Downs Way and includes the Neolithic causewayed camp of Barkhale south of the path.

Gumber Bothy has a National Trust camping barn at Gumber Farm.

(D) Stane Street

Built in the early years of the Roman occupation it connected Regnum (Chichester) with Londinium and was one of the most important highways in the south-east. Along it would have passed corn from the Downs, iron from the Weald and other goods from the continent. Built with hammered chalk and flints and topped with a flint and gravel surface only the raised central embankment, or agger, remains today.

Stane Street with the raised embankment, or agger, clearly visible.

(E) Cocking

A charming little village about half a mile north of the South Downs Way with footpath access away from the traffic of the A286. It is in Cowdray Estate country so many of the buildings are painted in the familiar canary yellow which seems to symbolise the estate's domain.

It has a number of pubs and B&B at:

Carters Cottage,
Cocking Causeway, Midhurst
Tel: 01730-814191
*Cycle storage, stabling and
grazing*

Josephine Longland,
Moonlight Cottage
Tea Rooms,
Cocking GU29 OHN
Tel: 01730-813336

🚶🚶 🚶🚶 🚶🚶

Section 8

COCKING to BURITON
14 miles (22.5km)

Continue up Middlefield Lane and once through Cockinghill Farm the Way begins a long steady climb along a smooth chalky track flanked on either side by a tall hedge.

At the cross-tracks keep ahead on the more obvious track which by now has become uneven and stony. There are good views to the left of Goodwood racecourse grandstand and the twin radio masts of the Trundle and as the Way begins to level

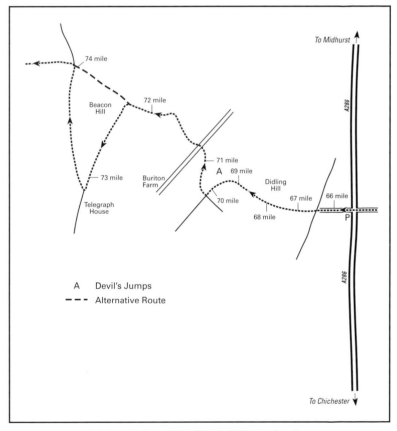

COCKING to BEACON HILL – 9 miles.

out the spire of Chichester cathedral can be clearly seen.

With the first sign of any real view ahead there is a trig point in the field on the right, followed by a derelict shooting tower with an even more precarious looking tower in the field opposite.

From here there are views over the Weald on the right. Keep ahead along the straight stretch over Didling Hill to enter woodland above Monkton House. This is a pleasant part of the Way, although it can be very muddy in wet weather because of the overshading.

Devil's Jumps (**A**) are on the right and shortly afterwards, at the next crosstracks on Philliswood Down, take an unexpected sharp right turn soon passing the tiny memorial on the right to Hauptman Joseph Oesterman, a German pilot who was killed during the Second World War.

The Way now descends to a T-junction, where turn left towards Buriton Farm, but only for a few yards before turning right along an enclosed path between two fences.

Follow the path round the edge of a small copse, taking great care for there are many unearthed tree roots.

Now there is an abundance of paths with numerous signposts over a fairly complicated section. Simply keep left in all instances as the Way begins the ascent of Harting Downs, soon to be followed by a steep descent before following the chalk path round left to take an apparent detour round the base of Beacon Hill.

There is a path straight over the top of Beacon Hill which is a strenuous climb, but more direct than the official route.

At the next T-junction turn right, a left turn leads to Telegraph House, built by Earl Russell, brother of the philosopher, Bertram Russell, on the site of the Admiralty signals station from which semaphore messages were sent during the Napoleonic Wars. Pass through a wooden gate beside a metal gate, and keep ahead along Bramshott Bottom as far as the mounted signpost.

Here the short cut over Beacon Hill descends sharply to rejoin the main route.

Turn left here, signposted Buriton, past a water trough and up quite a climb along a broad, smooth, chalky path which can be slippery in wet weather. Once the going levels out the green spire of South Harting church can be seen ahead with the radio mast on top of Butser Hill evident in the distance.

As the Way begins to climb again a fingerpost indicates a footpath off right to South Harting but there is an easier, quicker and more direct route a little further along.

Now the route seems to split in two but the more direct path is the right fork along which the cars in Harting Hill car park soon come into view. Keep to the path to the right of the car park, which soon emerges onto the B2141. Cross straight over the road, continuing along through the trees to the B2146 which also cross. Here a footpath keeps alongside the main road into South Harting **(B)**

The Way now continues along Forty Acre Lane, an enclosed stretch of broad, flinty farm track that runs almost level for two miles (3.2km).

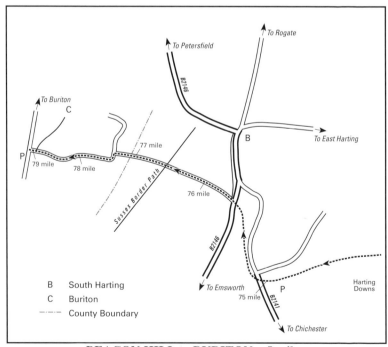

BEACON HILL to BURITON – 5 miles.

Looking from the Way towards the village of South Harting.

The Sussex Border Path crosses by Foxcombe Farm and, as a bridleway comes in from the left, the Way crosses the imaginary Hampshire boundary at Hundred Acres which, until it was extended to Winchester in 1989, marked the official end of the South Downs Way.

Turn left onto a metalled road by a magnificent copper beech, following the road round right past Sunwood Farm. Keep to the lane round left, where there is a sign to the right saying CART TRACK BURITON **(C)**.

> The cart track is also a footpath leading into the village which is a little under a mile (1.6km) away.

Follow the lane round right, past Coulters Dean Farm, then under the power lines where the metalled surface peters out and the familiar chalk track reappears. The route undulates through the woodland of Appleton's Copse before becoming a metalled road again on its descent to Newbarn Road and the Forestry Commission car park at Halls Hill.

A delightful bridleway leads off right here to Buriton arriving at the church and village pond.

POINTS OF INTEREST

(A) Devil's Jumps
A line of five Bronze Age bell barrows forming a spectacular group of large tumuli situated just to the right of the South Downs Way. For a closer inspection it is necessary to leave the main route by a little path through the trees to a site which makes an ideal spot for a picnic.

(B) South Harting
The first sighting of this attractive downland village is usually the green copper spire of its church but it has much of interest to offer including the remains of the village stocks and whipping post and the war memorial designed by Eric Gill.

Its most illustrious resident was Anthony Trollope, author of the Barchester novels, who spent the last years of his life here. The church, dating back to the thirteenth century, vies with that of Alfriston as the Cathedral of the Downs, and there are a number of timber-framed eighteenth century houses in the village.

Just south of the village is the National Trust property, Uppark, reached via the B2146 Emsworth road. Built around 1690, it retained all its original furniture and paintings until damaged by a disastrous fire in 1989 but has since been restored at great expense.

It was at Uppark in the 1880s that H G Wells' mother was housekeeper to Miss Frances Fetherstonhaugh, sister of Mary Bullock, the dairymaid Sir Harry Fetherstonhaugh married when he was in his seventies. The house appears in H G Wells' novel, *Tono Bungay,* as Bladesover and he describes his mother's days there fully in his *Experiment in Autobiography.*

Refreshments are available at the Ship and the White Hart.

South Gardens Cottages, South Harting, GU31 5QJ,
tel: 01730-825040, offers B&B and grazing facilities

The delightful village of Buriton – the original end of the Way.

(C) Buriton

Before the South Downs Way was extended to Winchester in 1989 this was journey's end. It is a pleasant, unassuming village with refreshments available at the Five Bells and B&B at:

The Old Hop Kiln,
Bones Lane,
Buriton, GU31 5SE
Tel: 01730-266822

Nursted Farm,
Buriton, GU31 5RW
Tel: 01730-264278

Section 9

BURITON to EXTON
13.25 miles (21.5km)

From the Forestry Commission car park at Halls Hill go through the gate and continue up the hill which rises steeply round to the left and into the woods.

At the Information Point fork right – riders fork left at this point – keeping ahead as far as the metalled road. Cross straight over the road keeping to the verge to the left and dropping down to the track through the trees at the first opportunity.

Continue ahead as far as the Cycle Hire Depot, where cross the road immediately before the Pay and Display kiosk, keeping to the public footpath alongside the car park to the Queen Elizabeth Country Park Visitor's Centre (**A**).

To leave the Country Park follow the footpath towards the bridge under the A3 where the bridlepath rejoins the main

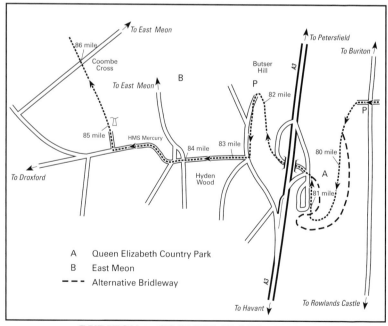

BURITON to COOMBE CROSS – 7 miles.

route. Cross the road at the end of the fencing, following the Way past Information Point 16 beside which are toilets for the disabled.

Bear left now across the Downs along an obvious route towards the radio mast on Butser Hill. Pass through a gate, keeping to the left of the mock Iron Age roundhouse which is the Information Centre, and cross the approach road to continue for about 100 yards before crossing back to keep ahead along a fenced path beside the road for half a mile.

When the fenced path peters out continue along the wide verge alongside a hedge on the left. There are good views to the left over Portsmouth Harbour, the Solent and the Isle of Wight and when the road swings off left take the lane to the right of the two lanes ahead marked with a sign UNSUITABLE FOR MOTORS.

This metalled road becomes a gravel road which, by the power lines, becomes the familiar gravel track. Now there is over a mile (1.6m) of fairly level country through Hyden Wood emerging at a crossroads, taking due care.

The Way continues straight ahead along the Droxford road to another crossroads about 100 yards further on. Keep ahead again with views of East Meon **(B)** church and village to the right, following the road round left past the main entrance to HMS *Mercury*.

Turn right alongside the perimeter fence and soon pass two radio masts at Wether Down where the route is back in open country again.

Descend steeply down a hard, sunken lane where the trees are close together and low hung – so riders and cyclists beware. At the metalled road is the tiny hamlet of Coombe Cross.

B&B and stabling available at the house of the same name.

The Way crosses straight over the road, kinking right then left at a carpet of wood chippings soon to turn left at the cross-tracks by the SDW fingerpost.

Continue down the concrete farm track to the road where turn right past Hall Cottages to turn left at the asbestos barn with the galvanised feed hoppers along the drive to Whitewool Farm. Cross the river and pass through the farm, turning right through the gate to continue along a concrete track in the direction of a disused chalk pit cut into the hillside. Turn right here, through another gate, and up a broad grassy track to reach the road. Once again walkers and riders go off in different directions. Cyclists and horses turn right at the road while walkers turn left.

In spite of lengthy negotiations a permanent route for this section of the South Downs Way across Old Winchester Hill and the Meon Valley has still not been agreed. Until such time as an official right of way is established **cyclists and riders** should

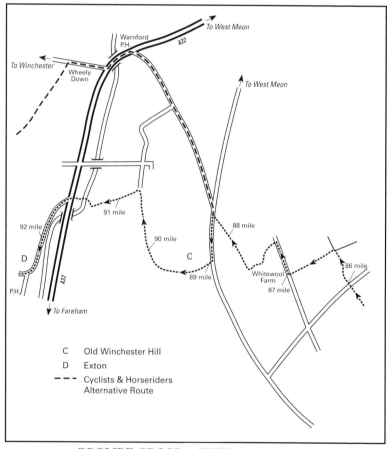

COOMBE CROSS to EXTON – 6.25 miles.

turn right and take the left fork into Warnford. At the A32, turn left past the George and Falcon public house, crossing the River Meon with its watercress beds, and once past Rose Lea Cottage follow the flint wall round right and continue along the road signposted WINCHESTER 10 MILES.

About 150 yards beyond Wheely Down House turn left at the public bridleway signpost beside the white weatherboarded building with the sign: FORGE ENTRANCE - CAR PARK. Here follow the gravel track, which soon bears right through a metal gate, before turning sharp left alongside a hedge on the left and up to a gate beside a five-barred gate. Continue along the track across the next field to another gate beside a stile, then through the woods to the road and a small car park. Turn right here to rejoin the main route.

Walkers, having turned left, may keep to the road or step into Old Winchester Hill Reserve (**C**), passing the two car parks to follow the Easy Going Trail at the Reserve's southern extremity. Pass through the gate by the sheep dip, follow the track round left, then right along a broad green sward past the trig point and direction finder on the left. Take the left fork in the direction of the SDW waymarker, over the stile and along an attractive woodland path.

Cut through the hedge at the marker post, turning right onto the track and left in 150 yards, passing under the old railway bridge where there is a choice of two levels of paths. Over the plank bridge and turn right, crossing the river to the A32, which cross into Exton (**D**).

Parking is available here.

Follow the road into the village, passing the church on the right.

POINTS OF INTEREST

(A) Queen Elizabeth Country Park
Covering an area of 1,400 acres and dominated by Butser, War Down and Holt Down hills this country park shows the contrast between dramatic downland and beautiful woodland. It is a

East Meon church.

naturalist's paradise and many Roman and Iron Age sites have
been preserved as Ancient Monuments within its confines.
There are also extensive networks of trails for walking, cycling,
horse riding or orienteering as well as designated areas for kite
flying, hang gliding and paragliding. Several barbecue sites are
available for hire suitable for family outings to group gatherings
and there are special events organised throughout the year. A
Visitor Centre and Cafe is situated by the main car park which
also houses a gift shop, information desk and toilets.

> Further information from Queen Elizabeth Country Park, Gravel Hill,
> Horndean, Waterlooville, Hampshire PO8 0QE Tel: 01705-595040

(B) East Meon

A beautiful village where Izaak Walton, author of *The Compleat
Angler,* first published in 1653, stayed to fish the River Meon
which runs under and beside the main street. The village is still
an important centre for trout fishing and has a fourteenth century
Court House which is occasionally open to the public.

Refreshments at the George public house.

B&B available in East Meon at:

Drayton Cottage	Dunvegan Cottage	Oxenbourne Farm
East Meon	Frogmore Lane	East Meon
GU32 1PW	East Meon	GU32 1QL
Tel: 01730-823472	GU32 1QJ	Tel: 01730-823239
	Tel: 01730-823213	Stabling/grazing
		facilities

(C) Old Winchester Hill

Surmounted by an Iron Age hill fort, its defensive earthworks dating from around the second century BC. It is now a nature reserve and as such certain restrictions apply. Currently these exclude entry to cyclists and riders of horses, although they may eventually be allowed access. It is maintained by sheep grazing so dogs should be kept on a lead at all times. Beside the trig point is a panoramic view finder and on a clear day the Isle of Wight and the harbours of Portsmouth and Chichester can be seen.

(D) Exton

A pretty village on the River Meon with a church dedicated to St Peter and St Paul. There was probably a church on the same site as early as the ninth century although the present one dates from about 1230. It was largely rebuilt in 1847 when it was closed for a year and the registers are complete from 1579. It has a remarkable headstone showing the angel of death summoning a scholar from his books and the inscription on it shows it was erected in memory of Richard Pratt of Preshaw who died in 1780.

Refreshments at the Shoe public house

B&B available in Corhampton, the village adjoining Exton, at Corhampton Lane Farm, Corhampton SO32 3NB.
Tel: 01489-877506

Section 10

EXTON to WINCHESTER
13 miles (21.1km)

Follow the road through the village, past the church, and as it bends left turn right by the SDW sign between Glebe Cottage and Bramcote House. At the stile beside the gate follow the field

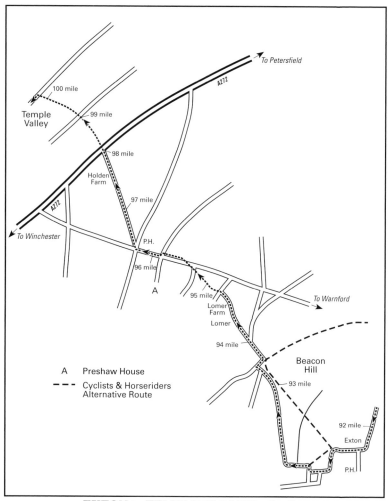

EXTON to TEMPLE VALLEY – 8 miles

edge along an obvious path as far as the next sign offering a choice of routes. The official route continues alongside the right of the hedge to rejoin the road at North Croft on its way up Beacon Hill. An optional alternative route – and a much better one – is to take the footpath diagonally across the next field which climbs Beacon Hill in almost a straight line until rejoining the road at a stile.

Just beyond a young plantation on the left there is a gap in the hedge on the right where a stile and a fingerpost offer the opportunity to cut off the corner in the road emerging in a small car park where the cyclists and riders rejoin the main route. There is room here to unbox a horse if necessary. The main route by road turns right just beyond the aforementioned stile to reach the car parking area at the next bend.

Keep to the road for about 275 yards (250m) staying ahead along a gravel track as the road swings off right. Trees line the path on the right on the approach to Lomer Pond which is visible through the foliage and then, on the left, just past Lomer Cottage the humps and bumps in the next field are all that remains of the lost medieval village of Lomer.

Follow the Way round left at Lomer Farm then right to turn sharp right again at the signpost just beyond the second cottage. Turn left again as the Wayfarer's Walk from Emsworth to Inkpen Beacon near Newbury joins the South Downs Way, and follow the farm track as far as a flint barn, where fork right to the road at Wind Farm.

Cross the road and turn left along a pleasant stretch of path which soon peters out to continue along the roadside where great care should be observed. The Way soon passes the impressive entrance to Preshaw House (**A**) and just beyond turns right at the cross-roads past the Milburys public house.

In about 200 yards turn left at the SDW signpost continuing ahead along Holden Lane by the barn as the road turns off right. The Way continues through Holden Farm to the A272 which cross straight over, passing through the gate and across the next field bearing slightly right to another gate where the way forward is self evident.

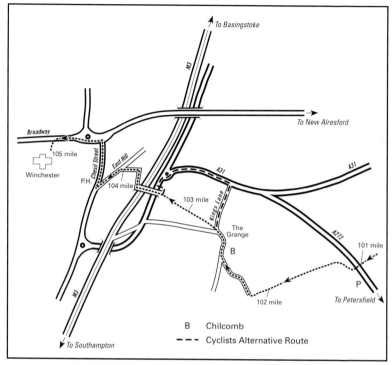

TEMPLE VALLEY to WINCHESTER – 5 miles.

Pass through a third gate before keeping ahead along an enclosed track to the road which cross before continuing ahead to where the Way meets a metalled road. Turn left here in the direction of the SDW signpost, past the farm and cottage to continue through the trees to the A272 where the Cheesefoot Head car park is a little way along on the left.

Cross the main road keeping ahead along a broad green track as far as the trees where turn right. A little way along this next stretch there are some good views over Winchester ahead.

At a point where the way ahead across a field seems to be the obvious route, the Way bears to the left, soon becoming a metalled lane and turning sharply down right by Little Golders, away from a flagpole and a sign warning of army ranges.

Follow the lane down into Chilcomb (**B**) and at the T-junction

King Arthur's statue in The Broadway, Winchester – and journey's end.

just past The Grange the route again differs for walkers and riders.

Walkers climb up three steps and over the stile to continue along a fairly long but straight path towards the busy M3 motorway. **Cyclists and horseriders** turn right along Kings Lane then left onto the A31. Left again at the roundabout to rejoin the main route over the M3.

The Way turns right once across the motorway keeping alongside for about 275 yards (250m) before turning left by a South Downs Way information board. Keep ahead past All Saints Parish Church, a substantial Victorian flint knapped building, bearing right at Michaelmas Cottage downhill at Petersfield Road and East Hill to the King's Arms and Blackboy's public house.

Turn right along Chesil Street and left at the roundabout to King Alfred's Statue in The Broadway, Winchester, the Saxon capital of England.

POINTS OF INTEREST

(A) Preshaw House

By the road, within the boundary of Preshaw House grounds, is Mill Barrows, an ancient burial mound which gives its name to nearby Millbarrow Down. The Fox and Hounds pub on the crossroads has been renamed Milburys. Inside is an old treadmill that used to draw water from a deep well cut in the chalk.

(B) Chilcomb

The early Saxon church is a little to the south of the village and still uses a bell cast in 1380. The old granary sits astride piles of stones to keep the rats out.

Complyns, Chilcomb, Winchester SO21 1HT offers B&B
Tel: 01962-861600

For accommodation in Winchester contact the Tourist Information Centre, The Guildhall, The Broadway, Winchester, SO23 9LJ. Tel: 01962-840500.

YHA Winchester Tel: 01962-853723.

SOME USEFUL ADDRESSES

The Ramblers' Association,
1/5 Wandsworth Road,
London SW8 2XX.
Tel: 020 7339 8500.

Society of Sussex Downsmen,
93 Church Road, Hove BN3 2BA.

South-East England Tourist Board,
The Old Brew House,
Warwick Park,
Tunbridge Wells TN2 5TU.
Tel: 01892-540766.

Sussex Downs Conservation Board,
Chanctonbury House,
Church Street,
Storrington RH20 4LT.
Tel: 01903-741234.

Youth Hostels Association
(England and Wales),
8 St Stephen's Hill,
St Albans AL1 2DY.
Tel: 0870 870 8808.